# Virginia

by the Capstone Press
Geography Department

**Reading Consultant:**
Bruce Twyman
Advertising Director
Virginia Tourism Corporation

CAPSTONE BOOKS
an imprint of Capstone Press
Mankato, Minnesota

Capstone Books are published by Capstone Press
151 Good Counsel Drive, P.O. Box 669, Mankato, Minnesota 56002
http://www.capstone-press.com

*Library of Congress Cataloging-in-Publication Data*
  Virginia/by the Capstone Press, Geography Department.
  p. cm.--(One Nation)
  Includes bibliographical references (p. 45) and index.
  Summary: Gives an overview of the state of Virginia, including
  its history, geography, people, and living conditions.
  ISBN 1-56065-503-8
  1. Virginia--Juvenile literature. [1. Virginia.]
  I. Capstone Press. Geography Dept. II. Series.
F226.3.V57 1997
975.5--dc20

                                                    96-35113
                                                       CIP
                                                        AC

Photo credits
Lynn Seldon, cover, 6, 18, 28
Flag Research Center, 4 (left)
FPG, 25, 26; A. Schmidecker, 4 (right)
Unicorn/Jean Higgins, 5 (left); Doris Brookes, 5 (right)
James Rowan, 8, 34
Root Resources/Lia Munson, 10
William Folsom, 12, 30
Jean Buldain, 16, 21, 22, 32

# Table of Contents

# Fast Facts about Virginia

**State Flag**

**Location**: In the mid-Atlantic region of the southern United States

**Size**: 40,598 square miles (105,555 square kilometers)

**Population:** 6,872,912 (1999 U.S. Census Bureau estimate)
**Capital:** Richmond
**Date admitted to the Union:** June 25, 1788; the 10th state

**Cardinal**

**Flowering dogwood**

**Largest cities:**
Virginia Beach,
Norfolk, Chesapeake,
Richmond,
Newport News,
Arlington, Hampton,
Alexandria,
Portsmouth, Roanoke

**Nickname**: Old
Dominion; Mother
of Presidents
**State bird**: Cardinal

**State flower**:
Flowering
dogwood
**State tree**:
Flowering
dogwood
**State song**: "Carry
Me Back to Old
Virginia" by
James A. Bland

**Flowering dogwood**

5

# *Chapter 1*

# Colonial Williamsburg

Visitors to Virginia's Colonial Williamsburg can step back into history. Colonial Williamsburg has been carefully rebuilt. It looks just as it did during the 1700s. More than 100 buildings have been restored. They include homes, shops, and the jail.

Visitors tour Colonial Williamsburg's Capitol and Governor's Palace. They eat and drink in the old inns. They buy goods made by present-day Williamsburg crafters. They see how colonial Americans lived and worked.

**Colonial Williamsburg has been carefully rebuilt to look just as it did during the 1700s.**

**The Revolutionary War's last battle was fought at Yorktown.**

### Early Williamsburg

In 1699, Williamsburg became the capital of the Virginia colony. A colony is a group of people who settle in a distant land but remain governed by their native country. The English governors of the colony lived in the Governor's Palace.

Williamsburg became the capital of the state of Virginia during the Revolutionary War

(1775-1783). The first two state governors also lived in the Governor's Palace. They were Patrick Henry and Thomas Jefferson.

## Historic and Beautiful

Virginia has many historic places. Jamestown was the site of the first permanent European colonial settlement. The Revolutionary War's last battle was fought at Yorktown. The Civil War's first battle was fought at Bull Run in 1861. The Civil War ended at Appomattox in 1865.

Eight presidents of the United States were born in Virginia. For that reason, some call Virginia the mother of presidents. Today many of their homes are open to visitors. George Washington's Mount Vernon and Thomas Jefferson's Monticello are favorites.

Virginia is also a beautiful state. Wide bays and sandy beaches lie along the Atlantic Coast. Inland, the Appalachian Mountains sweep across the state. Forested hillsides line the Shenandoah Valley.

# Chapter 2
# The Land

Virginia is known as a mid-Atlantic state. It lies on the coast of the Atlantic Ocean. Virginia's lowest point is sea level. This is found along the Atlantic Coast.

Virginia is also a southern state. Five southern states border Virginia. They are Maryland, West Virginia, Kentucky, Tennessee, and North Carolina. Washington, D.C., borders a small part of northeastern Virginia.

Mountains cover much of western Virginia. The middle of the state has a high, rolling plain. A flat, sandy plain covers eastern Virginia.

**The Blue Ridge Mountains rise in western Virginia.**

**Wild horses live on Assateague Island off Virginia's coast.**

## The Tidewater Region

Eastern Virginia is called the Tidewater. Ocean tides flow into Chesapeake Bay. They also flow into the Potomac, Rappahannock, James, and York rivers.

Chesapeake Bay divides the Tidewater's land. A peninsula called the Eastern Shore lies east of the bay. A peninsula is land surrounded by water on three sides. Many islands are near the Eastern Shore. The largest one is Assateague Island. Wild ponies and snow geese live there.

Mainland Virginia is west of Chesapeake Bay. The Great Dismal Swamp lies to the south. Cedar and cypress trees grow there. Many kinds of birds and snakes live there.

Lake Drummond is in the Great Dismal Swamp. It is Virginia's largest natural lake.

## The Piedmont

The Piedmont covers the middle of Virginia. The name Piedmont means "foot of the mountain." Mountains rise west of the Piedmont's hilly land.

In the eastern Piedmont, rivers flowing southeast form waterfalls. This is called the fall line. Richmond was built on the fall line. It is the state capital.

The Piedmont's river valleys have rich soil. Farmers in the river valleys raise tobacco, peanuts, and livestock.

## The Blue Ridge Mountains

The Blue Ridge Mountains begin west of the Piedmont. Mount Rogers rises in the southern Blue Ridge. This is Virginia's highest point.

Mount Rogers reaches 5,729 feet (1,718 meters) above sea level.

Shenandoah National Park is in the northern Blue Ridge Mountains. There, limestone rocks look like chimneys and bridges. Forests of hickory and oak cover the hillsides. Deer, bears, and bobcats live there.

## Appalachian Valley and Plateau

The Great Appalachian Valley lies west of the Blue Ridge. The Shenandoah Valley is part of this great valley. The Shenandoah River flows through the Shenandoah Valley. Apples and grains grow well there.

The Appalachian Plateau forms Virginia's southwestern corner. Forests cover the land.

At the southwestern tip of Virginia is the Cumberland Gap. Thousands of pioneers traveled west through this mountain pass.

## Climate

Virginia has mild weather throughout the year. The Tidewater has the warmest weather. It also

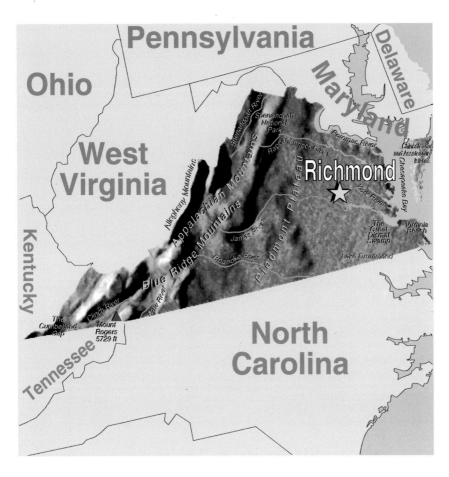

receives the most rain. A small amount of snow falls on the coast in the winter.

The hills and valleys of the west are cooler. In winter, the mountains receive up to 30 inches (76 centimeters) of snow.

# Chapter 3
# The People

Virginia has the 12th largest population of all the states. Four Virginia cities rank among the nation's 100 largest cities. They are Virginia Beach, Norfolk, Richmond, and Newport News.

Today, about 70 percent of all Virginians live in cities. More than half of them live between Arlington and Norfolk.

## European Backgrounds

About 77 percent of Virginians have European backgrounds. Their families came from England, Scotland, Ireland, Wales, Germany,

**Virginia Beach is one of the nation's largest cities.**

**17**

**Virginia Governor L. Douglas Wilder was the first African-American governor in the United States.**

and France. English people settled in eastern Virginia in the 1600s.

In the 1700s, many Scotch-Irish and Germans moved to Virginia. They made homes in the Shenandoah Valley and Blue Ridge. Some of their families have kept the old customs. For example, Galax has a night of mountain music each month. People sing old folk songs. Clog dancers wear wooden shoes.

French and Scottish immigrants also arrived in the 1700s. Immigrants are people who come to another country to settle. Many settled in the cities of the Piedmont and Tidewater.

## African Americans
The first Africans were brought to Virginia in 1619. They worked as indentured servants. This means they worked without pay before gaining their freedom. After seven years, they were freed.

In the 1640s, Africans were brought as slaves to Virginia. They worked on Virginia's tobacco plantations. A plantation is a large farm. In 1661, Virginia made slavery legal.

Virginia's slaves were freed in 1865. Hampton University was founded in 1868 in Virginia. Many African Americans have gone to school there.

In 1900, Virginia passed segregation laws. These laws meant that African Americans had to stay apart from white Virginians.

Segregation became illegal in 1954. Since then, Virginia's cities have elected African Americans as their mayors. In 1989, L. Douglas Wilder was elected as Virginia's governor. He was the first African-American governor in the United States.

Today, about 19 percent of Virginians are African Americans. In Richmond, Jackson Ward is the main African-American business area. Church Hill is a large African-American neighborhood.

## Native Americans

By the 1700s, few Native Americans lived in the state. New settlers had driven them off the land.

Today, about 15,000 Native Americans live in Virginia. They belong to the Chickahominy, Monacan, Mattaponi, Nansemond, Pamunkey, and Rappahannock tribes. Most live in small towns.

The Chickahominy hold a powwow each September. It is held at Providence Forge.

## Hispanic Americans

About 2.5 percent of Virginians are Hispanic Americans. Many live in the state's large cities.

Hispanics speak Spanish or have Spanish-speaking backgrounds. More than 32,000 of Virginia's Hispanics are from Mexico. Large numbers of Virginia's Hispanics also come from El Salvador or Puerto Rico.

About 15,000 Native Americans live in Virginia. The Mattaponi wear traditional costumes at special times.

## Asian Americans

Another 2.5 percent of Virginians are Asian Americans. The largest number of them came from the Philippines, Korea, China, and India. In recent years, many have also come from Vietnam.

Most Asian Americans live in Virginia's cities. Some own shops or restaurants. Others work for the government.

# Chapter 4

# Virginia History

Native Americans arrived in Virginia about 5,000 years ago. By the 1600s, the Powhatan, Monacan, Manahoac, and Cherokee lived there.

## European Settlement

In 1570, Spanish missionaries arrived. Missionaries are people sent to do religious or charitable work in a territory or foreign country. They built a settlement on the York River. Disease and Indian attacks quickly killed them.

English explorers then claimed the region. They named it Virginia.

English colonists landed in Virginia in 1607. They built Jamestown on the James River. This

**Jamestown was the first English settlement in North America.**

was the first permanent English settlement in North America.

John Rolfe, a Jamestown colonist, began planting tobacco in 1612. Soon tobacco became Virginia's biggest money-making crop. In 1619, the House of Burgesses met in Jamestown. This group of leaders passed laws for the colony.

## The Revolutionary War

England had 13 colonies in North America. In the 1760s, England placed heavy taxes on the colonists. Virginia's Patrick Henry called for freedom from English rule.

Leaders from each colony met in Pennsylvania in 1774. Virginia's George Washington became head of the Continental Army. Another Virginia citizen, Thomas Jefferson, wrote the Declaration of Independence. The colonial leaders approved the declaration on July 4, 1776.

For the next five years, Washington's army fought the British. In 1781, the British surrendered at Yorktown, Virginia. This ended the Revolutionary War.

**Thomas Jefferson wrote the Declaration of Independence.**

**The South surrendered at Appomattox in 1865.**

### The 10th State

Virginia's James Madison helped write the
Constitution of the United States. A constitution
is the basic law of a colony or state. Virginia
approved the Constitution in 1788 and became
the 10th state. Richmond was the state capital.

Washington was the first president of the
United States (1789-1797). Other Virginians
later served as president. They were Thomas
Jefferson, James Madison, and James Monroe.

Virginia planters grew tobacco, cotton, wheat, and other crops. African slaves worked on large plantations. They planted and harvested crops.

## The Civil War

Slavery was not allowed in the North. Virginia and other Southern states still used slave labor in 1860.

Virginia left the United States in 1861. It joined 10 other Southern states that were also for slavery. They formed the Confederate States of America. Richmond became the capital of the Confederacy.

In April 1861, the Civil War began. More battles took place in Virginia than in any other state. In 1865, the South surrendered at Appomattox.

## Reconstruction

The war destroyed many Virginia cities, farms, and plantations. Virginia's harbors, roads, and railroads were also ruined.

Virginia also lost several western counties. These counties became the state of West Virginia in 1863. The people there had not wanted to leave the United States.

**Shipbuilding grew in Virginia to become a big business.**

After the Civil War, Virginia underwent Reconstruction. This means Virginia reorganized and reestablished itself. A new state constitution was written. It gave African Americans the right to vote. Virginia then reentered the United States in 1870.

### Growth and Challenges

In the 1880s, textile and furniture factories opened in Virginia. Shipbuilding grew. Coal was found in southwestern Virginia.

In the early 1900s, Virginia's African Americans lost many rights. To vote, they had to pay a poll tax. Many African Americans could not pay the tax.

## World Wars and Depression
The United States entered World War I in 1914. Langley Air Force Base opened near Hampton. The war ended in 1918.

The Great Depression (1929-1939) hit the country. Many Virginia factories closed or slowed down. Workers lost their jobs. A drought in 1930 ruined many Virginia crops. A drought is a long period with no rain.

The United States entered World War II (1939-1945) in 1941. Virginia made weapons for the war. Battleships docked at Newport News.

## Modern Virginia
Since World War II, more industries have been started in Virginia. Chemical, clothing, and computer companies have moved to the state.

Some factories have polluted Chesapeake Bay. Virginians are working to clean up the bay. They are also trying to protect the Eastern Shore.

Virginians take pride in their long history. They also look ahead to a bright future.

# Chapter 5
# Virginia Business

Virginia has a healthy economy. About 75 percent of Virginia's workers are service workers. Many of them work for the government. Others work in tourism. Making goods, farming, and mining are other important jobs in Virginia.

## Service Industries

Government and tourism are large service industries in Virginia. Many Virginians work in United States government offices. The Pentagon is in Arlington County. The Central Intelligence Agency (CIA) is near McClean.

The Central Intelligence Agency is located near McClean.

**Fishing boats in Chesapeake Bay catch oysters to sell.**

Tourists spend about $10 billion a year in Virginia. Hotels, motels, and restaurants receive much of this money.

## Manufacturing

Chemicals are Virginia's leading manufactured goods. They include nylon and medicines.

Tobacco products are also very important. Cigarettes and pipe tobacco are made from Virginia's tobacco crop.

Many Virginians build boats and ships. Newport News Shipbuilding is the world's largest privately owned shipbuilding yard. Norfolk and Portsmouth also have shipbuilding yards.

Making foods is important in Virginia, too. Peanut butter and Smithfield hams are leading foods. The Eastern Shore has many poultry plants.

**Agriculture and Fishing**

Tobacco is still Virginia's most important crop. Most of it is grown in the Piedmont. Virginia farmers also grow corn, soybeans, peanuts, and apples.

Farmers in the Piedmont raise cattle, hogs, and poultry. Some farms also raise horses.

Fishing boats in Chesapeake Bay catch crabs, oysters, and clams. Some small fish farms in Virginia raise trout.

**Mining**

Virginia is a leading coal-mining state. Miners work underground in southwestern Virginia mines. Crushed stone and limestone are other important Virginia minerals.

# Chapter 6
# Seeing the Sights

Virginia has something for everyone. Sandy beaches line the Atlantic Coast. Trails lead visitors through Virginia's forests and mountains. Revolutionary War and Civil War battlefields lie throughout the state. People visit homes of former United States presidents.

## Tidewater Virginia

The Tidewater area has many historic sites. Jamestown was Virginia's first settlement. Today, no one lives in Jamestown. However, visitors can see the foundations of many Jamestown homes.

**Arlington National Cemetery is one of the sights to see in Virginia.**

Nearby is Jamestown Settlement. A Powhatan Village has been rebuilt there.

Exact copies of three ships sit nearby on the James River. The original ships brought the first English settlers to Jamestown.

North of Jamestown is Williamsburg. Visitors enjoy walking through this rebuilt 1700s town. The College of William and Mary is also in Williamsburg. It was founded in 1693. Today about 7,500 students attend classes at the college.

Nearby is Busch Gardens Williamsburg. European villages from the 1600s have been recreated there. Busch Gardens also has more than 30 thrilling rides.

Berkeley Plantation is west of Williamsburg. The first Thanksgiving was celebrated there in 1619.

Southeast of Williamsburg is Yorktown Battlefield. Visitors can walk along the trenches built by British troops.

Virginia Beach is on the southern coast of the state. This is Virginia's largest city. Visitors enjoy its 28 miles (45 kilometers) of sandy beaches. They swim, boat, and surf.

## The Eastern Shore

Visitors can reach the Eastern Shore from Virginia Beach. They take the Chesapeake Bay Bridge-Tunnel. This is the longest bridge-tunnel in the world.

On the east side of the Eastern Shore are many islands. They include Assateague and Chincoteague islands.

Assateague Island is home to wild ponies. The first ponies arrived 400 years ago. They were believed to have survived a shipwreck.

Each July, many ponies are rounded up. They then swim across to Chincoteague Island. There they are sold. The money goes to the Chincoteague fire department.

## Northern Virginia

Mount Vernon stands in northeastern Virginia. It overlooks the Potomac River. This was George Washington's home. Visitors can walk through the house and the grounds.

Arlington National Cemetery is north of Mount Vernon. More than 200,000 people are buried there. The Tomb of the Unknowns is guarded 24 hours a day. The graves of President John Kennedy and his wife, Jacqueline, are there, too.

## The Piedmont

Richmond is south of Arlington. It has been Virginia's capital since 1780. Thomas Jefferson designed the Virginia State Capitol.

The Maggie Walker House is also in Richmond. Walker was the first African American to run a bank. She was also the country's first woman bank president.

Charlottesville is northwest of Richmond. The University of Virginia is there. Thomas Jefferson founded and designed this school. Today, about 18,000 students attend classes.

Outside Charlottesville is Monticello. This was Thomas Jefferson's home. It appears on the back of the nickel. Jefferson designed and built it.

South of Charlottesville is Appomattox Court House National Historic Park. That is where the Civil War ended. Visitors can stand in the room where General Robert E. Lee surrendered. He was the leader of the South's Confederate Army.

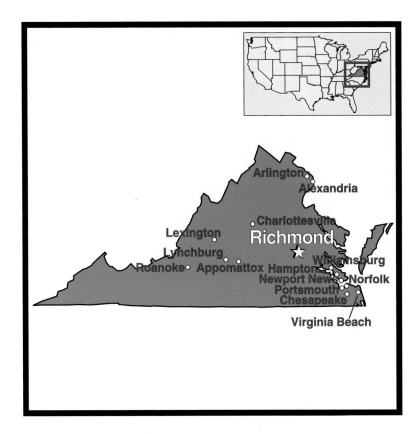

## Western Virginia

The Blue Ridge Mountains are in northwest Virginia. Shenandoah National Park is in the Blue Ridge. Many visitors go to Skyline Caverns. One room in this cave looks like a capitol dome.

Southwest of the park is Lexington. This was Thomas "Stonewall" Jackson's hometown. He was a Confederate general. Lexington is also the home of Virginia Military Institute. Jackson taught there before the Civil War.

# Virginia Time Line

**3000 B.C.**— The first Native Americans reach Virginia.

**A.D. 1570**—A group of Spanish missionaries build a small settlement in Virginia.

**1607**—The first English settlers land at Jamestown.

**1674-1676**—Nathaniel Bacon leads a rebellion against the colonial governor and fights for rights of people in western Virginia.

**1693**—The College of William and Mary is founded in Williamsburg.

**1736**—Virginia's first newspaper is published in Williamsburg.

**1776**—The 13 American colonies declare independence from England; Virginia adopts a constitution.

**1788**—Virginia becomes the 10th state.

**1831**—Nat Turner leads a slave rebellion and is caught, tried, and hanged.

**1861**—Virginia leaves the Union and joins the Confederacy of Southern states; the Civil War begins.

**1865**—The Civil War ends at Appomattox when Confederate General Robert E. Lee surrenders to the Union forces.

**1870**—Virginia is readmitted into the United States.

**1904**—Virginia passes the poll tax, which prevented many African Americans from voting.

**1928**—Virginia passes a law against lynching which is to murder someone by a mob.

**1959**—Virginia begins to integrate its schools.

**1964**—The Chesapeake Bay Bridge-Tunnel opens to traffic.

**1971**—Virginia adopts a new constitution.

**1977**—Richmond's first African-American mayor, Henry L. Marsh III, is elected.

**1990**—L. Douglas Wilder becomes Virginia's and the nation's first African-American governor.

**1995**—*Inc.* magazine names Virginia a good place to do business.

**1996**—Virginia Military Institute (VMI) votes to allow women to attend; archaeologists find remains of the first fort in Jamestown.

# Famous Virginians

**Arthur Ashe** (1943-1993) Pro tennis player who became the first African American to win the U.S. Open (1968); born in Richmond.

**Willa Cather** (1873-1947) Writer of novels; won a Pulitzer Prize in 1922; born in Winchester.

**William Clark** (1770-1838) Explorer of the land of the Louisiana Purchase with Meriwether Lewis; born in Caroline County.

**Ella Fitzgerald** (1918-1996) Jazz singer who won eight Grammy Awards; born in Newport News.

**Patrick Henry** (1736-1799) Revolutionary War patriot who said, "Give me liberty or give me death"; born in Hanover County

**John Paul Jones** (1747-1792). Naval officer during the Revolutionary War, who said, "I have not yet begun to fight."

**Robert E. Lee** (1807-1870) Leader of the Confederate army during the Civil War and president of Washington and Lee University (1865-1870); born in Westmoreland County.

**Meriwether Lewis** (1774-1809) Explorer of the land of the Louisiana Purchase with William Clark; born in Albemarle County.

**Shirley MacLaine** (1934- ) Actress who won an Academy Award in 1983; born in Richmond.

**Pocahontas** (1595-1617) Daughter of Chief Powhatan; her marriage to colonist John Rolfe brought some peace between the Powhatan and the colonists; born near Jamestown.

**Powhatan** (1550?-1618) Chief of the Powhatan Indians in eastern Virginia; father of Pocahontas

**William Styron** (1925- ) Novelist who won a Pulitzer Prize in 1967 for *The Confessions of Nat Turner*; born in Newport News.

**Fran Tarkenton** (1940- ) Pro football quarterback; holds many passing records; born in Richmond.

**Booker T. Washington** (1856-1915) Freed slave who founded Tuskegee University in Alabama in 1881; born near Roanoke.

**George Washington** (1732-1799) First president of the United States (1789-1797); born in Westmoreland County.

# Words to Know

**colony**—a group of people who settle in a distant land but remain governed by their native country

**constitution**—the basic laws of a country or of a state

**drought**—a long period of no rain

**immigrant**—a person who comes to another country to settle

**indentured servant**—someone who must work without pay for a number of years before gaining his or her freedom

**missionary**—a person sent to do religious or charitable work in a territory or foreign country

**peninsula**—land that is surrounded on three sides by water

**plantation**—a large farm

**population**—the number of people in a place

**powwow**—a Native American gathering with traditional clothing, dances, and foods

**segregation**—a policy of keeping people of different races separate

**surrender**—to give up

textiles—cloth, or the yarn used to make cloth

tourism—the business that provides services such as lodging and food to travelers

trench—a long, deep cut in the ground that protects soldiers during battle

# To Learn More

**Barrett, Tracy.** *Virginia.* Celebrate the States. Tarrytown, N.Y.: Benchmark Books, 1997.

**Blashfield, Jean F.** *Virginia.* America the Beautiful. Chicago: Children's Press, 1999.

**January, Brendan.** *The Jamestown Colony.* We the People. Minneapolis: Compass Point Books, 2000.

**Joseph, Paul.** *Virginia.* United States. Minneapolis: Abdo & Daughters Publishing, 1998.

**Ruskin, Thelma.** *Indians of the Tidewater Country of Maryland, Virginia, Delaware, and North Carolina.* Lanham, Md.: Maryland Historical Press, 1997.

# Useful Addresses

**African American Heritage Tour**
710 Settlers Landing Road
Hampton, VA 23669

**Appomattox Courthouse National
  Historical Park**
Route 4, Box 169
Appomattox, VA 24522

**Luray Caverns**
P.O. Box 748
Luray, VA 22835

**Marine Corps Air-Ground Museum**
Marine Corps Combat Development Command
Quantico, VA 22134

**Monticello**
P.O. Box 316
Charlottesville, VA 22902

**Mount Vernon Estate and Gardens**
George Washington Memorial Parkway
Mount Vernon, VA 22121

# Internet Sites

**Excite Travel—Virginia**
http://www.excite.com/travel/countries/
  united_states/virginia

**Travel.org—Virginia**
http://travel.org/virginia.html

**Welcome to Virginia**
http://www.state.va.us

**Williamsburg Online**
http://www.williamsburg.com

# Index